This book belongs to:

____

Made in the USA
Coppell, TX
20 April 2023

15850645R00066